The Way 2

The Way 2

Poems by

Peter Waldor

© 2021 Peter Waldor. All rights reserved.
This material may not be reproduced in any form, published,
reprinted, recorded, performed, broadcast,
rewritten or redistributed without
the explicit permission of Peter Waldor.
All such actions are strictly prohibited by law.

Cover design by Shay Culligan
Cover Image: "antique manuscript page of unknown origin"

ISBN: 978-1-63980-043-8

Kelsay Books
502 South 1040 East, A-119
American Fork, Utah 84003
Kelsaybooks.com

for Lisa again

Books by Peter Waldor

Door to a Noisy Room

The Wilderness Poetry of Wu Xing

Who Touches Everything

The Unattended Harp

State of the Union

Gate Posts With No Gate

Nice Dumpling

Owl Gulch Elegies

Unmade Friend

Something About the Way

Contents

I

Pink David	15
Pink David	16
Aubade	17
The Bardo	19
The Last Oozings	21
Eggs	26
Flock of Sheep	27
Ships Passing in the Night	28
Instructions for Lovers	29
All Symbols Day	30
Shards	31
Lingerie	32
Ancient House	35
Instructions for lovers	36
Jealousies, Etc.	37
Neat Firsts	38
Breath	40
The Anguish of Love	41
Breakfast	42
Beautifully Lovely	43
Pink David	44
Pink David	45

II

Pink David	49
Pink David	50
Rear Entry	51
Untalked About	52
Waiting Room	53

Casting Couch	55
Mysterious	56
XXX, Etc.	57
An Old Man's Lovers	68
All Night Long	69
Faked Orgasm	70
About Bondage	71
Leaving	72
It's Not a Cliffrose	73
Cheaters	74
Glow	75
You Build Your Own Path	76
Pink David	77
Pink David	78

III

Pink David	81
Pink David	82
Two Kisses	83
Pale Vermillion	84
The Buddha	85
Loves of Lives	87
Borscht Or Yes Yes	88
Stained Glass	91
Wild Tending	92
Laying the Terrible Groundwork	93
The Friendship of Old Lovers	94
Telescope Chute	95
What We See	96
Affective Touch	98
Clams Oraganata	101

Scars	103
Two Frog Sounds	105
Gold Kettle Fly	107
French Kiss	108
William Blake	109
Pink David	110
Pink David	111

I

Pink David

A pink David
at the back
of the atelier,
just his head
and tendoned
neck, on a shelf,
lost in jewelry,
cheeseboards
and coasters.
A life size head,
unlike the amplified
Uffizi rendition.
At first I thought
it was a certain
slant of light
but now I see
he really is pink
and it's not Carrara
or even Indiana
marble but styrofoam,
beautiful word.

Pink David

Imitation is the least sincere
form of flattery but this David
would make the other reproductions
jealous and what more sincere form
of flattery is there than jealousy?

Aubade

You lift a pair
of underwear
from your great pile
of clothes, faded pink
and white striped,
hold them on your palm,
like a stone
you found in the desert,
then lift them to your face
for a big inhale,
perhaps to smell
a trace of your own
tangy juices,
or the lavender
of the detergent,
or nothing other than
the loveliness
of underwear,
cottony and thin,
but not so thin
they are translucent,
and not so insubstantial
that they have been
reduced to a string
trussing up the anus.
They will conceal
and reveal just the right
amount, and they
are comfortable.

You fold and leave
them on top
of the pile
until you rescue
them and pull
them up your legs.

The Bardo

Remember that moment
in 1980 when every poet
in America was jealous
of the Stafford poem
about finding the dead deer
on a road, stopping, feeling
the body and noticing that
there was a baby in its belly
whose heart was still beating;
he hesitated then rolled the deer
off the road into a ravine.
That poem is
yesterday's newspaper,
last year's nest;
no one memorizes it now
to impress a lover or teacher,
but tonight I remember
the poem as you stop
on a dangerous mountain road
and get out to pull a dead deer
to the shoulder. We don't see
the injuries in the dark.
It looks healthy except
when we drag it away
we notice the loose neck
and before we leave it
on the shoulder
you gently adjust its head.
Even though it's no longer
with its body anymore
you wish it well through
the Bardo and like Stafford

before us you hesitate
before we leave, suggesting
we strap it to the roof,
take it home and butcher it,
but we are vegetarians
and our freezer is small
and other unspoken
considerations, including
laziness and I yell at my
son to stay in the car
but he gets out anyway.
Alone with the deer,
he whispers a prayer.
He can't help himself.
He is the last priest
left in the world,
patient on the dark road.

The Last Oozings

Today I learned
to use your apple press.
I turned the large wheel
of the masher and the
small wheel of the press,
using a piece of scrap rebar
to gain leverage.
Since I am so weak
I pretend to be strong,
even stating my anxiety
that I turned the wheel
so hard I was about to crack
the board that was pressing
the apple bits into the
bottom of the barrel.
It's best not to overload
the chute that feeds
the masher so I finally
learned to feed the apples
one at a time, one at a time,
as creatures are born
into the world.
You spun the heavy
wheel slowly, a fine spray
and occasional bits flew
out of the mashing chamber
and your arm was drenched
and sticky, and I had unwanted
thoughts of blast radiuses,
and I wanted to lick the stuff
off your dark forearm.
You used two shims
to tilt the machine

so the last oozings poured
out of the groove more quickly
into the stainless bowl.
The machine is not old
though with its heavy
elegant parts it could
have come out of one
of the early forges.
A gift from your ex-husband.
He bought it when a neighbor
and dear friend who had
shared her old press around
the neighborhood farms
stopped sharing for
whatever reason and so
the world was a little less
collective and I wonder
if you and your family
and your new machine
in those happy autumns
were the beginning
of a new collective,
a fresh act of generosity
replacing one that vanished.
Your own orchard was
too young to provide
enough apples so we
picked without asking
from a neighbor's orchard.
You said, years ago,
the old widow who owned
the place told you
to take what you want

and don't even bother
asking in the future.
We are taught from
an early age not to steal
from old ladies but you
reassured me and a series
of hard frosts were upon us
so the unpicked apples
would spoil anyway.
The froth was like seafoam
and we licked it off
our fingers when the other
was looking away,
it being unsanitary.
I don't know why it's called
canning instead of jarring,
but we ended up at the end
of the afternoon with
sixteen gleaming jars
of apple cider, and a small
bag of apples that were
so perfect we couldn't
bear to drop them
in the chute but rather
set them aside for human
teeth; perhaps a little
girl who gets lost in
the forest and yearns
for sweetness and hydration
will take one out of
a witch's hand.
I love how quietly
you yell at your daughter

to keep the canning pot
at 180 degrees for
thirty minutes and she
looked at you with a look
that said she remembered
that lesson for twenty years
already and every lid
was indeed pressure sealed,
no rejects; these jars
could rest a thousand years
in an Egyptian tomb
and be fresh for the
archaeologist who
dusts them off.
I love how the same daughter
names the farm animals
and treats them lovingly
before they are slaughtered.
I was afraid the large pigs
would eat me when I
entered their pen with
a bucket of apple pressings
and I did feel a pig's teeth
when it licked me
and touched its snout
against the back of my palm.
Who knows if it doesn't
know more of its fate
then we do of ours.
At last I leave these words
on top of a pile of
a thousand post cards

you wrote to
voters in Florida.
You only asked them,
in misplaced humility,
to *please vote,*
and not to vote against
the putative dictator.
I wish you could have
sent each one a jar
of apple cider.
Unspoken is your hope
that they vote for
the liberal candidate,
for to be liberal is to be
open, free, kind,
and, yes, conservative,
that is, not to use
too much water when
you wash dishes or shower,
not to tear up too many
plants when you replace
your septic tank, not
to make too many
assumptions about people
you meet in life,
and to help them
any way you can.
You said every family
could live for a year
off two cultivated acres.
And yes, there is enough
land on earth for that.

Eggs

You are out with friends
and I secretly prepare
eggs over easy and sautéed
broccoli, your ex-husband's
favorites, which you won't
eat anymore. I suppose I
should seek help to find out
why I would do such a thing.
I hope I don't have to talk
to a stranger for twenty
years to find out.

Flock of Sheep

Not everything has changed.
You still try to climb faster
than your partners, so I am
losing sight of your hair
streaming over your pack
like a flock of sheep streaming
down Blackface Mountain.
I know you are simply trying
to subvert the patriarchy
and enjoy some competition.
I hate competition but I
concur about the patriarchy.

Ships Passing in the Night

I wake up when you go to sleep and when you wake up
I fall asleep, our ships always passing at that darkest
time of night, but they are lucky, old paddle wheelers
and a ship hand from the one going from Lake George
Village up to Bolton Landing saw a lantern on the other
ship and motioned his friend the captain for a full stop
and the two crews gathered at their railings to talk for
five minutes, the most profound conversations, mostly
about the weather, full of theories and predictions.

Instructions for Lovers

Run your index finger
slowly down
your lover's spine,
rising and falling
between crenellations;
then after the spine ends
continue down below,
ever slower like a runner
at the end of a long race
who finally is sure
she will cross the line,
slow and determined
and with no shame.

All Symbols Day

All Symbols Day is in similar
spirit as All Saints Day
except on All Symbols Day
we don't embrace symbols,
we try to leave them behind.
I happened to be in the wilderness
on the big day, looking for
a shrine where lovers
leave stone hearts but since
I couldn't find the shrine
I left my stone heart
in a dry riverbed where
it must wait for a flood
to spin it and carry it
where it was meant to go.

Shards

We stumble on an old
miner's camp, picking
up objects,
the lid to a lamp
that said *Ideal Inspector
Lamp,* a governor
valve with size stated
one and three-quarters,
a shoe sole rolled up
like a tortilla.
You are not a treasure hunter
but you collect a handful
of scattered spikes,
leave them in a neat pile,
and you collect the shards
of a broken purple jar
and leave them in a pile,
and you leave the site
with just one small
piece of quartz,
something the mountains
themselves coughed out
of their clogged veins,
the sort of thing
a miner could carry
away without a
foreman hassling him.

Lingerie

Visiting Berkeley, California
to help with home hospice
for your dying aunt
we take a couple hours off
to visit the neighborhood
lingerie shop, looking
for a bottom and a top
that are scant, cotton,
not so different from
"normal" underwear,
but different enough
to make all the difference.
I, a man and you,
a woman, confer happily.
I wonder if the idea
for lingerie has
been with us back
to the early hominids.
Did the cave woman
place a rabbit pelt
over her crotch
and the cave man
press his hand
against it before
tossing it over
a stalagmite?
Did the man ever
dress like that?
As a small boy,
searching through
my parents' closets,

I found my father's
large pile
of neatly folded
cotton undershirts,
and his silky old
boxer underwear.
My mother had
a considerably
larger area, underwear,
panty hose, night
gowns. There was
definitely some
sense of fashion,
but no stockings,
no lingerie. I wonder
if I missed
a secret compartment.
The sales clerk asked
us why we were
in Berkeley; somehow
we didn't tell her,
the conversation turning
to how long it would
take to walk to the water,
restaurants along
the way, and the dainty
items we picked which
happened to be the
young woman's
personal favorites.
She placed it all in
tissue paper and then
a gleaming bag
we'll save for other gifts.

The items themselves,
I'll reach through time
and lay them in my
mother's quiet drawer.

Ancient House

You are up all night
in your dead son's shirt,
in the ancient family home.
On the edge of your infinite
wound, you choose life,
love and adventure.
You've cut the shirt's neck
wider and put a groove
in the front as well.
You say it's ok,
these all-night tears.
I wish I was there
to hold you,
with, don't worry,
nothing to say.

Instructions for lovers

This time you get to be a rag doll,
only respond to the direction
of the other, what the other says,
or letting the other move your
body and intuiting and responding
to the requested movements,
typically the hand moving or directing
the other's hand, but it could be anything.
You could be asked to drag your palm
from your knee up to your center
or your lover could take your
palm and do the same.
Then, of course not the same night,
not even the next night, for this is
not a quid pro quo; but another
night a season away,
switch rolls, for even if this has
nothing to do with equality,
there is equality with true lovers.

Jealousies, Etc.

My wise friends have
decried my many petty
jealousies, sexual and
otherwise, but how
delightful, how you
first tell me you are
going into the wilderness
with the tall handsome
young man from the
the house around
the corner and I say
sounds wonderful
without a hint of irony
and then you say,
by elaboration
you are going with him
and his partner.
I wonder if you are
somehow instinctively
trying to allay my fears,
or else, get me thinking
about the wild ménage
à trois in store for you,
unrolling a couple
sleeping pads
on a bluff looking
towards the peaks.

Neat Firsts

Shameful how careless
use of language perpetuates
misogyny. Yesterday,
for example, in an offhand
way while talking
about lunch I said
I didn't want any
sloppy seconds and I
immediately regretted
you heard me use such
ugly words, but you chose
to ignore them, turning the other
cheek as you so frequently
do with me, and indeed,
the world. Could you even
be trying to give me
the benefit of the doubt,
that I had neutered the term
from its gender charged
past and therefore redeemed it?
That if it had a sexual etiology,
it wasn't gendered and therefore
lost its ugliness—of a man
being with a woman who
was recently with another man.
After all, fear of disease
transmission aside,
what's the difference
anyway, relating
to the order of partners?
All the many genders
and their combinations
should also be irrelevant.

And the corollary must
be discredited as well,
that is, Neat Firsts,
that is, in the extreme,
being with a virgin.
Would any man
or woman, for that matter,
now, knowing what we
know these days,
seek a virgin for
his or her partner?
Maybe you didn't even
hear what I said,
you just naturally tuned
out my shameful
language and here I am
rubbing salt in an
old wound, by mentioning
what I said again.
But when I went
into all the gory
detail you agreed
and said it would
indeed be
awfully slimy.

Breath

Your sleeping breath
on my arm,
the inhalation
undetectable
but the exhalation
puffs like an
old locomotive,
bending my arm hairs
with each breath.
We all want to sleep
soundly but how
lucky I am to be
the one awake,
watching.

The Anguish of Love

My hand on your chest,
over your heart,
and your hand on top
of mine, clasping it,
I think because you love
me and then I wonder
if it's because you don't
want me to caress
you freely and when
we fully awaken
and exchange thoughts
I tell you the reasons
why I think you were
clasping my hand.
You said I was right
on both counts
and I grimace
with the anguish of love.

Breakfast

I love how
when I am still
in you, or,
more properly,
you are still
around me,
we start talking
about breakfast,
for example,
do we have any
milk left for
French toast,
I don't know,
let's make it
anyway.

Beautifully Lovely

Two holes are better than one,
one large on the left hip
of your long underwear,
and one small at the center
of your purple panties.
A hand can enter the first hole
with fingers spread
as if measuring a span
but the second hole
is only passable
by the index finger,
unless the finger tires
and the tongue provides
some relief. Both holes
are by accident
and by design as are
all presences and absences.

Pink David

The underworld is
as it is in a child's
fantasy; one rule is
demons can only
move when
no one is looking.
So it is with David,
the tell-tale sign—
each morning he is
looking out a different
picture window
of the atelier.
One morning facing
south, the next west.
Another rule
is adults never notice
the demons, they think
the child is silly or worse
when they say the stuffed
bear is not a bear
and moved from a shelf
to a stool in the dark room.
I must be childlike
because I notice
David's transit;
and I know demons
make exceptions
to the rule,
at the end when
they lose their shyness
and flash at you
with gnashed teeth.

Pink David

He moves to every window
as if searching for
a way out. As we pass
we don't see David
but he sees us.
It's not us looking
at art but art looking at us.
He is not gazing over
our shoulder to Rome
in a glare of defiance
but merely looking
intently at a potential
lover, as we all are.
Nor is he the young
King of Israel or
even a Florentine youth.
He is my father
looking at my mother
at the Newark,
New Jersey Department
of Motor Vehicles,
for the first time.

II

Pink David

A damsel fly in distress
wanders around the closed
atelier, it doesn't understand
glass and keeps trying
to pass through the silica
sheets until it collapses
into a dark and dusty cleft
in David's pink curls.

Pink David

He's not bad really,
he could be a cross
between a young
Marcello Mastroianni
and Omar Sharif.
I'm sure the sculptor
was thinking of the stars,
not the anonymous
Florentine youth
of his fantasies,
a young man who
at the time was
sewing some last coins
into his jacket before
making for the border.

Rear Entry

One hand on your back
the other wrapped around your chest
and pulling you into me
as if someone else or a wind
were trying to pull you away,
as I enter you from behind.
Afterwards you said it was
"relaxing." First I was happy,
for what greater gift can
one give to another then
to help them relax?
Naturally I had second thoughts.
Should I take it as the highest
compliment that you relaxed?

Untalked About

Are some things better
left untalked about.
Why ask your love
what she dreams of
when you make love?
The answer might not
be you or even
a meadow filled with
wildflowers. I wish
I dreamed of others
when we make love,
but if I am not simply
consumed by our passion,
if my mind does wander,
it wanders to you,
though you could be
a little different
in my mind's eye,
you might be wearing
a frilly soft shirt,
its clam shell buttons
half undone,
and/or you might stink
from two weeks
in the wilderness
with just a hint
of old perfume.

Waiting Room

An expectant mother was
frightened by her first
contraction and rushed
to the hospital where you
greeted her, first peeling
and washing the flour
and dough from her fingers
which she had forgotten
in the rush; you wash
slowly so you had
a chance to talk, to get to
know her, set her at ease,
on your rolling stool,
your knees at 10 o'clock
and two o'clock,
your strong thighs
under your scrubs.
I can't wait to slide my palm
up from your knee and pause
half-way, like one sliding a
hand up a railing, while I
think of a good question.
Perhaps it will come
to me now.
I am in the waiting room
with the expectant mother's
relatives and friends,
all whispering hopefully,
waiting while time is stopped.
I am the only one waiting
for you, the midwife,

it's sad the waiting room
isn't also full of your friends.
There will be no fresh
fry bread tonight or tomorrow
in that busy home.

Casting Couch

In pornography there is
a major subgenre called
the casting couch.
I am not innocent but I
hadn't heard of it.
One male actor plays the film
director and one female actor
plays a woman there to audition
for a role in a porno film.
The director, of course, puts
the auditioner through the paces
while he holds a video camera.
As I said, I am not innocent but I never
heard of casting couches
until, in the back alley
I was carrying a couch
to my office and a friend
yelled *casting couch?*
And I did some research
so I wouldn't seem stupid.
Of course we would be better
off without pornography
but until then at least
the actors could switch up
roles and those of us imitating
them could also switch,
one and then the other
holding the camera, directing.
Always switching roles
until not playing any at all.

Mysterious

There is that clicking whistling intake sound
you make with your breathing before
you power your chop saw and lower it
on the far edge of your gray guideline,
pausing for a moment to kiss me
earnestly even if your mind is on
complications related to the next measurement,
and when you bend deeply to retrieve
a screw there is a slice of your archaic
torso visible between your shirt and your jeans
and I even see inside your jeans to the frayed
label which I mistake for the top edge
of your underwear, washed and worn
so many times it's thinned to lingerie;
but there are very few things
about you that I mistake. I know you
want me to know you well but to
still be a mystery, but worry not,
for the more I get to know you the more
mysterious you become.

XXX, Etc.

1.

Love and desire—those twins.
Will they grow up to be best friends
or the most different siblings in the world?

2.

Nothing worse than a self-confident white man
with a sense of humor and hint of vulnerability.

3.

There are no more newspapers in these
outlying towns and driving through you notice
five flags at half-mast and you are afraid.
The space between encampments more
likely desert scrub than farms.

4.

Let's say you were first generation Russian
and I was third generation Ukrainian
and we met at a parlor.   Would we
marry and live ever after?

5.

I am so afraid you love me but I am
just the next cardboard character
you chance by to pour your
heart and soul out to and when
you find out I am, alas, just cardboard,
you won't be happy.

6.

How you ripped someone's shirt off in a bar,
the snaps sounding like rain drops on a thin roof,
recounted to me to make me suffer, of course,
and I was delighted.

7.

Do all lovers bristle at being the lover
and all beloveds yawn at being the beloved?

8.

It is too unbearable to wash
my shirt after you wore it.

9.

Are all my revelations superficial and all your
non-revelations full of depth?

10.

Of course it would be far better to be
with you in the flesh but there are
consolations in dreaming.

11.

Why do it that way if it doesn't give you pleasure, sitting up?

12.

Be nice to fall into a routine with you,
breaker of all my routines.

13.

If you left me in an unexpected way
would I be crushed or would I be
ecstatic, like someone given a
life sentence but was just freed
from the prison of love after already
serving some time?

14.

Is slight concealment a primal directive or a culturally developed
imperative?

15.

The profound sadness that comes from watching great dancers.

16.

At first your intelligence dazzled me,
now I am merely jealous.

17.

When I apologize to you for objectifying you sexually,
you say "it's ok dude."
Still, I better think about it.

18.

I throw my shirt against your angry goddess.

19.

How easy it is to help you,
how hard to let you help me.

20.

At the National Park, after looking at the dinosaur bones,
on the way out, you slip our brochure back into the plastic bin.

21.

We let each other love one another,
like leaving our doors unlocked
in a dangerous city, no one
would think to try the handles
because it's way too risky
to leave them unlocked.

22.

Funny how people are always whispering
about other people being lovers.
It's always a mix of malice and prayer.

23.

You wrap your hair
in a knot as you go down on me
so you can see and I can see,
unless our eyes are closed.

24.

Could unethical non-monogamy be more ethical
than ethical non-monogamy?

25.

When with some self-doubt I ask you,
sincerely, why you love me, I cringe
when you answer *because you are a poet*.
I fear, one day, you will hate me
for that occupation.

26.

Whenever you describe the worst qualities
of your old lovers or husbands
I think you are describing me to a "T."

27.

Embarrassed that
I let you,
with your hand,
guide me into you,
embarrassed I didn't
find my own way.

28.

To have sex with
children in the house
the door must be closed.
The door is open now.
If I close it it means
you will know what I
am dreaming of
so I don't know
what to do.

29.

I love how you scratch your head
before making love,
like a mathematician
at the blackboard before
solving a problem.
It's good to scratch an itch
before doing anything important,
even if the itch doesn't exist.

30.

We both think our own
hands are ugly.
Does everyone
think their hands
are ugly, like their voices?
And then we say
we think the other's
hands are beautiful.

31.

You like to keep your light on
a while before you go to bed,
in hopes of making love
with visibility?

32.

In Germany together, speaking Gaelic and reeking of garlic.

33.

Let's meet each's other.

34.

Just a little tushy hanging out below
the angled short jean shorts.

35.

If we had two other lovers in bed with us
and our backs were to each other while
each of us made love with one of the other
lovers our buttocks could rub against each other.

36.

I said *I can't hear you*, so quietly
you couldn't hear me say it.

37.

Lovers lie abed with quiet breath
of wakefulness, neither touches
the other or talks, both pray
this is not a bad sign but just
respecting the other's solitude.

38.

My love sees hearts everywhere.
My friend insisted his wife empty
their house of all the stone hearts
she collected over the years.

39.

You take a battery out of your vibrator
and put it in your outdoor grill.

40.

When you abruptly lift off me
my semen falls out of you
onto my chest, a milky crescent
scar where there was no wound.

41.

We fall asleep to the sound
of a bed creaking in the next room,
speeding up before the silence,
while you read to me about
skunk cabbage also known as
Parson in a Pillory, either the last
flower of winter or first of spring.

42.

Afraid of frightening our neighbors
above, below and on either side,
you muted your wild growl of delight
to a barely audible purr and afterwards
your voice was raspy, nearly gone.
If you had roared as usual, I'm sure
your voice would be fine now.

43.

After reading the essay
Ten Tips for Better Blowjobs
you go down on me.
I couldn't help but laugh
as you counted off each tip
with your fingers but then
I was very serious.

44.

You don't like it
when I praise you.
Once you said
it's just fucking
when I said
*you are a miracle
worker.*

An Old Man's Lovers

Many of the old man's lovers
came to his funeral.
They had suspected each other existed
and were glad to finally meet,
in a corner of the parlor,
away from his family,
laughing over his absurdities,
how he only liked the bottom,
how he couldn't go to the bathroom
in their houses, how he was
allergic to cats, to name a few.
Many friendships began.

All Night Long

Once I walked for
twenty-four hours
and no one said I was
exaggerating when
I told the story
but no one will believe
I went down on you
and you fell asleep
which wasn't an insult
and I stayed down there
with my hummingbird
tongue all night
so when you woke
I was in the same
place humming
and it worked

Faked Orgasm

I fake an orgasm
for my love
only because she is
the love of my life
and I know it
makes her happy
to hear me
beside myself.
My sound effects
were like two old
trees rubbing
together high up
in the canopy.

About Bondage

The terrible, beautiful,
counterintuitive truth
is the one tied down,
ankles and wrists
cinched to the old
Amish bedposts,
leather straps on the ankles,
silk on the wrists,
that one may be in control
and the one free of restraints
may be the one
submitting
to the orders of the other.
She could be cracking a whip
or tickling with a feather,
no matter.
I guess this is obvious.

Leaving

My love dreams of leaving me,
of going far away,
and she is quick to point out
she also dreams of returning
and that she loves me.
I say it's ok, who wouldn't
dream of leaving their love,
especially if it's a true love?
Leaving with little money,
a daypack with a novel,
sweater, cap, and poncho,
standing on the on ramp,
sticking out a hopeful thumb.

It's Not a Cliffrose

There is a flower
one expert called a cliffrose
but it's not
and another expert
called a gardenia
but she knew
it was not;
anyway, I saw you walk
through a grove of these flowers,
too beautiful to look at
so, I averted my gaze;
bushes full of the pale blossoms
with the yellow center,
each of the four petals
curled at the end
like a piece of parchment
that had just been unrolled,
their fragrance,
with a breeze blowing our way,
at dusk,
was overwhelming enough
to make us stop doing
whatever we were doing
or thinking.
Since we are human
we broke
off a sprig to take home
to put in your grandmother's
small vase
but we noticed the sweet aroma
vanished completely
as soon as
we snap the slender stem.

Cheaters

Cheaters always prosper.
I find one cheatgrass seed
lodged in the broadloom
I should double bag it
and send it to the dump
but I blow it off my palm instead
like a shy butterfly
onto the meadow
I remember you slowly
picking the cheatgrass seeds
out of my shoes in the wilderness
the seeds were hooked and woven
into my shoes and socks
then you scrubbed
the poison ivy off for I
had wandered through
cheatgrass and poison ivy
You said you weren't susceptible
but the next afternoon
below your thumb at the ancient
Chinese pressure point
a rash was blooming
You said it was nothing
but I saw you turn away
to scratch the itch and I
walked away in restored shoes
Of course I said thank you
but I don't think I know
how to say thank you

Glow

I love how you touch wildflowers,
like an awkward grandmother
fluffing a boy's hair,
like someone gliding their hand
across a railing who doesn't
need it for support,
like someone at the ocean's edge
just touching the surface,
like someone smoothing the top
of a warm folded sheet; no, none
of those, it's just you, so gently
the flowers are not worse
for the wear and your hand
glows along with the rest of you.

You Build Your Own Path

You comb the forest
for smooth stones to take
home for your path,
taking only ones that had
already been dislodged,
leaving the others like so many
queens and kings in their dirt thrones.
Once you let me help you roll
a large stone uphill and since
it wasn't a Greek myth
the stone stayed where we left it.
The path must be smooth.
The path must be crooked.
It must have at least one bridge.
The rules.

Pink David

If I had the guts
to steal the Pink David,
perhaps when the
proprietor was talking-up
a couple from Texas,
I wouldn't find some
celebrity I wanted
to ingratiate myself with
to pass it to, the way
Apollinaire gave Picasso
the Mona Lisa after
he stole it; I'd place
the light pink head
in an avalanche path
and yell for a trigger.

Pink David

Styro(s) sounds like
the Greek island where
non-binary gender
identification is the norm
and foam sounds like
the root of seafoam
rolling onto the
sands of Styros.
Extruded or chiseled
or carved by wind
or waves, what's
the difference,
it all urges us
on to love.

III

Pink David

My brother once told me
I looked Roman and should be
an action movie star.
Now I look like an old Jew.
If styrofoam were an
accessible medium of the day
Michelangelo would have
picked it instead of the stone.
After all David's particular
block was rejected twice
before M. took it on.
Imagine if we were only
rejected twice in love.

Pink David

I thought styrofoam
was only good to hold
tea and liquid nitrogen.
David moves and changes
everyday, today he's resting
on a carton, with Hindu influence,
rings and a sagging chain
connecting nostril to ear.
Is he for sale
or merely a prop?
One afternoon he had
a beige corduroy cap
tipped to the side
like a buoy in a wake,
and I bought the cap
for my son thinking it
could help if he were
inclined to romance.

Two Kisses

I know a man who as a 5-year-old
shared a passionate kiss with the girl
of his dreams; he then had to wait
another 52 years for another
passionate kiss, this time with
the woman of his dreams
(a different person than the girl.)
I tell you this, you in despair,
so you know sometimes one
must wait, for every reason under
the sun and no reason at all.
That man's first kiss was as long
as it takes to pull a hand off
a hot stove, the second is still
taking place, lasting as long as
a mountain eroding
away by the wind.

Pale Vermillion

You don't notice
or even mention the two
bruises on your biceps
where you held and moved
armfuls of split wood
into your wood pile.
You know how serious
it is to eat or use plant
or animal life.
There is nothing more
beautiful than a healing
bruise, after one day
changing from purple
to pale vermillion.
Sometimes I like to pin
you by your biceps,
but today I start at
the wrists and slide
to the hands,
palm on palm
so our prints,
our uniquenesses,
are against each other
and we further engineer
lips, tongue and breath.
What isn't unique
after all, even if only
modestly so.

The Buddha

Your friend carried
the photograph of the Buddha
deftly down her dark stairs,
holding it with both hands
so she couldn't use the railing,
and leaned it against an old
magazine rack on top
of an old round table,
in the basement, by the bed
she made for us,
for you, her old lover, and me.
I am grateful for all she's done
for you, forever grateful,
and grateful, though perplexed,
she never gave herself
completely to you.
I did not receive
her kind blessing.
I see the picture hook
in the bathroom where
she removed the Buddha,
the humble brad shines
on the wood panel,
perhaps the brad itself
is a representation
of the god, still smiling on all
the urinating humans,
the ones who stand up
and the ones who sit down,
but I imagine the chubby man
was happy to be lifted
and moved to the basement,
perhaps he'll stay a while,
blessing the underground,

his gold leaf flaking off,
rust showing beneath.
Who knows why gods
are more beautiful
covered with rust.

Loves of Lives

How strange it must have felt
when the love of your life
rejected your advances and told
you if she succumbed she would
lose herself amidst the passion
and she was too afraid
to let that happen.
Was it an act of domination?
For if she had let herself go
and you were unyielding lovers,
you would have been equals,
you would no longer be the one
looking up to the other.
I wish she were braver,
even if it meant I never
would have met you,
the love of my life, or we
would have shook hands
and talked for five minutes,
by chance, at a summer barbeque.

Borscht Or Yes Yes

After a few days separation
we are in each other's arms,
a little shy and overcome
by desire. Just as the
vestige of shyness
was vanishing you notice
a spider on the wall,
noiseless and patient,
effortlessly holding
its vertical position
through some elegant
evolutionary mechanics
and you get up to
find a jar, which the
spider drops into easily
and you take it downstairs
and free it into the
chilly autumn evening.
And since there must
always be another reason,
you have remembered
the borscht which you had
set to cool on the porch.
You dug up the beets
that afternoon and wanted
to make the soup
quickly while the sunlight
was still fresh in the
gnarled roots.
I thought of my grandmother's
borscht fifty years ago,

simmering in her oval
iron pot, the sliced brown
bread. She didn't
seem to have any vestige
of her Byelorussian
peasantry, except
for that soup and bread.
I don't wonder where
she is now,
but I wonder where
the soup pot is.
That's a failure of wonder.
I was afraid, old man
that I am, that by the time
you ventured back with the
empty jar I would have
lost my ability to make love,
but it wasn't so,
I slowly worked you
through your maroon
underwear. Since we
had the house to ourselves,
we could say what we wanted
to say or moan what
we wanted to moan,
yes and yes,
though I could only
moan because your
engorged clitoris
was in my mouth.

One palm
and fingers were
assisting my tongue
and the other was up
on your chest,
wondering if that
was simply too
much stimulation
for you, so plying
gently. You had said
someone you know
was bitten by
a daddy long legs
and I said I learned
from my children
daddy long legs
could be deadly,
a jarring fact,
given how as children
we thought them
the most amiable
of spiders.
You disputed the deadliness.
You have slipped
your hands in my
armpits and pulled
me up, for it is time
to be deep inside you
and no place else.

Stained Glass

With a realtor
in an Edwardian
full of molding
and stained glass,
but creaking.
In the attic,
a room, a chamber,
with a rack, whips,
whips with studs,
mirrors everywhere,
enough handcuffs
to arrest a large protest.
The realtor closed
the door quickly.
It's true domination
is violent, but would
the world be a more
peaceful place
if we all had a
secret attic room?
I followed the realtor
out, slipping a pair
of handcuffs in my
pocket, but there
was no key.

Wild Tending

My love waits
until the flowers
shrivel up
and she harvests
the seeds, crumbling
them into her hands
and carrying them
to seed a fallow
spot in the wild.
I cut flowers
before they go
to seed, place them
in a vase for
a few days and then
I put them in a plastic
bag destined for the dump.

Laying the Terrible Groundwork

Pathetic as it sounds
I was desperate for you
to tell me I was your
greatest lover and then
at just the right
unbearable moment
you told me so.
Of course, I had laid
the groundwork,
telling you the same
the day before,
so you had
little choice,
it just took you a day
to work yourself up to it.

The Friendship of Old Lovers

Early and no time to make love
since my love is leaving to go
back country skiing with her
old lover. Still, old lover or no,
I tease her for a few minutes
so she'll dream of returning
to me and my hand that moves
gently, slowly, to the top edge
of her inner thigh. It's like
the edge of the world
in those dark ages maps
where it says
Where there be dragons.
I want her to be excited
to come back to me,
but what if,
excited, by accident,
the two of them make love?
They are on the
Commodore Run
at Red Mountain,
where experienced skiers
have been lost. Risk of love.
Risk of death.
Of waiting.

Telescope Chute

We fall asleep with no news
about whether your old friend
was caught in the big
Telescope Chute Avalanche.
I remind you to call his friend
in the morning, but no news.
The skiers used the same
path the miners took
up to the Camp Bird Mine.
My jealousy seems like
a petty thing now as we walk
up Hope Lake Road. Snow
blows across so the road just
seems like a natural clearing.
We walk quietly, it's early
evening now and still no news.

What We See

I say I saw a quadruped
then you say you saw an Elk.
Then I saw the Elk.
Then you saw a female Elk.
Then I saw the female.
You looked for and
found its newborn
hidden nearby.
I didn't see the baby
but saw the mother
moving away and
returning,
moving away
and returning,
with ever widening
radiuses.
You saw the mother
trying to decide
whether to abandon
its child because
of the threat we posed,
across the gully.
I saw the indecisive
mother but I had no
idea it was us,
and I still couldn't
see the baby.
You said let's get
out of here quickly
and don't use your
clattering sticks,
then maybe the mother
might return.

I moved quickly
and quietly as I could.
When we made it to
the far side of the ridge,
out of hearing,
I wanted to continue
away but you wondered
if Elk mothers ever return
in a situation like this.
You wanted to sneak
up to the ridge
to see if mother
and child were reunited.
I wondered what you
were thinking and asked
if we haven't done
enough damage.
I am slow but
eventually I get it.

Affective Touch

I don't know why but the two
of us weren't talking, on a
wilderness trip. My son
was with us. Your daughter
and son-in-law were also
part of our small group;
they flipped their raft
and nearly drowned.
The group pulled over,
stunned, then it hailed
as we setup camp, hailstones
the size of wild strawberries
and the group put them
in their stiff drinks.
Just down river you led me,
naked, into a cold eddy.
Every few seconds
a ripe mulberry floated by
in the counter current,
and we ate them out of the
water, ignoring the impurities,
each giving the other what
we found. We dried off
in the river breeze and you
led me to our tarp and pulled
me on top of you. We started
talking again after that.
We tried to explain
to each other, why,
despite it being obvious.
The love-making happened
so fast and yet I, at least,
still seem to be on that tarp,

free, but worried my son
would surprise us and a
passing boat might
take our picture.
In the Garden of Eden
a snake convinces
the lovers to eat the
forbidden fruit.
We walked up river
and found a mulberry tree.
There was a rattlesnake in
the clefted trunk; it was
forbidding us from
picking, but the canopy
of branches was so wide
we were able to shake
a mother lode of mulberries
into our upturned umbrella.
My son's cheeks were
stained deep purple;
he'd be embarrassed
if we had a mirror,
but I don't tell him,
rejoicing in the few days
we can't see ourselves.
There were other fruit
trees, peaches, walnuts,
seemingly wild, but a
collapsed wall and overturned
trough meant someone
tended the trees, not
long ago. In the tent
you read a bedtime story
about a witch-healer,

my son and I
on either side of you,
when your daughter
zipped herself in,
in tears, distraught
about the accident
and that her husband
would take her into
such danger, you held
her and said "it's going
to be ok baby," your
baby in her 30s now.
My son and I did our
best to fall asleep
quickly so we wouldn't
overhear the quiet
conversation. I woke
when your daughter
left and you stroked
my arm. Somehow
I was full of desire
again and you reached
down with your hand
and held me, I was
content that was all
that would happen,
you holding me
as I fell asleep again,
my son on the other side,
the 31,000 cfs river
a static radio.

Clams Oraganata

No need to say the clams
were killed before their time, shells
striated, perhaps a sign of age,
like tree rings or wrinkles or forgetfulness.
They were split open and the sides
with the meat were covered with bread crumbs,
olive oil, lemon juice, finely cut fresh parsley,
garlic, and of course, oregano,
then flash baked
and served six to an order, the empty
shells clicking in a sack like cicadas
and my exuberant father ordered
three orders for our small family
along with chicken savoy, ziti with pot cheese
and linguini with more clams.
We were semi-law-abiding middle class
Jews so naturally we took great delight
dining at the Belmont Tavern next to
friends and lieutenants of the DeCavalcante
and Gambino families, long before
they were crushed by the FBI, Russians and Chinese.
We took great delight in the way
they threw down the plates like frisbees,
refused to take dessert orders even
though it was on the menu and once
refused to serve two clam dishes in one meal.
Once my friend at Cornell Hotel Management
School took his whole class to the Belmont
so they could scratch their chins
and ask just what is hospitality?
Floor to ceiling photographs—
Stretch, the owner/chef with a giant lobster,
Joe DiMaggio, of course,

with a giant grin, boxers in silk robes
and young men who couldn't
be alive anymore even if they survived
their glamorous lives.
And once, forlorn, love lost, I went alone
and sat at the bar, next to Jimmy Durante's
twin and composed a feeble farewell letter.
It went like this…I fear I have offended you
somehow, my apologies if so, and my apologies
for dropping by unannounced.
Could we talk for a few minutes, you could
sit on the couch, I at the table? Maybe we
could have each learned a little more.
Farewell, be happy, good luck.
And once, the day before my mother died
I promised to take her to the Belmont
that night but then we were too busy
and I told her one day soon instead
and I worried she could die before that
and then she died before that,
that night, in fact.
She was a strong woman and if anyone
could carry anything to eternity
she could carry the flavor of
clams oraganata. We did get to go
a few months before.
Stretch was long dead and his daughter
Annette had taken over; her gruffness gone,
she shocked us and sat down
at our table and asked questions
about my mother's grandchildren.
My mother wasn't surprised.

Scars

Scars grow with age
as I notice on a tree
I've passed for years.
At first the claw marks,
which I surmised
were raccoon claws
and bear claws, were,
years ago, thin as an ink
line coming from a
slow moving quill pen.
Now, years later, the
scars are two fingers
wide. My father would
ask for two fingers when
offered a stiff drink.
I give my friend who
was court martialed
for desertion
but now grows faro
in Oregon, an ironic
two finger salute,
both of us smiling
at his four working
limbs. My love has
a scar and I try
to help her
forget the pain
and remember
pleasure. I slide
two fingers down
from her collar bone,
down and into her,

gently but with force,
in and out and she
helps, moving and
moaning.

Two Frog Sounds

Of course our science and technology
will destroy us, but today at dusk
my love and I walked towards an intermittent
pond and from a distance the frogs were croaking
in a full-throated chorus, it sounded like
a hundred ratchets spinning at once in a giant
repair shop and there seemed to be waves
in the sound. Instead of just enjoying the moment
I took out my multi-function device and recorded
a few seconds. Naturally we walked closer,
wanting more, to be more intimate with the music,
and the frogs stopped speaking for we must appear
large, ugly and dangerous. The hair on their
hairless necks told them, beware.
We edged back a few feet and two or three
began croaking again. We could hear
each voice with only the few in action
and they could be talking. It seemed
more beautiful that way. The first larger
sound and these small sounds made me
think of the community and the individual,
even of Thespis stepping from the chorus.
How much we need the chorus and the
one or two to step from it now and then.
We walked away holding each other
because we were cold and we loved
one another. Later we listened
to the device and we could hear
our breathing along with the clicking
of the gleaming ratchets and, at first,
I cursed the technology for being
too sensitive, but then relaxed
and remembered we were, indeed,

breathing. The frogs heard, I am sure.
I'd like to tell all those wet princes
and princesses we could be human
examples in their frog museum.

Gold Kettle Fly

My love went to brush a hair
off the back of her neck;
instead she fractured the wing
of a gold kettle fly and despite
her coaxing it wouldn't fly
off her palm; she didn't cry
but sighed for the way
people are in the world.
A long time ago,
in grammar school,
boys would sneak
behind one another and slap
the back of each other's necks.
I thought the worst of them
but maybe some of them
are sighing, living in gentleness,
doing something about injustice,
mending broken wings.

French Kiss

We kiss,
mouths slightly open
and a snow flake
falls in and melts
on our touching tongues.
The snowflake is unique,
but we are like
everyone in the world
looking for love.
The snowflake fell
a great distance,
slowly, thanks to
the pillows of air,
but it never reached
earth thanks to the
wet heat of love.

William Blake

After wandering around
in a fit of late-night insomnia
I slip back in bed cooled
by the night air,
where my love,
white hot, in the midst
of a hot flash, pulls my
cool body against her,
which works temporarily,
for without contraries
there is no progression,
as I always say, I, William
Blake, without being sure
of what it means.

Pink David

I'll carry him away
under my elbow
in some wax paper,
like an olive bread.

Worthless or worth a lot—
all the same
on the Egyptian scale.

Let sex workers
in the brothels of paradise
eternally rest.

Pink David

Caucasians
are more accurately
pink than white.
Imagine not just the
pink styrofoam head
as a prop for some
earrings, but the whole
body pink as a peeled
grapefruit, just past
adolescence, lazy,
on a daybed.
Amazing how young
lovers can think of
things other than love.

About the Author

Peter Waldor is the author of eleven books of poetry, including *Door to a Noisy* Room which won the Kinereth Gensler Award from Alice James Books, *Who Touches Everything,* which won the National Jewish Book Award and *Gate Posts with No Gate,* which is a collaboration with a group of visual artists. Waldor was the Poet Laureate of San Miguel County, Colorado from 2014 to 2015. His work has appeared in many journals, including the American Poetry Review, Ploughshares, the Iowa Review, the Colorado Review, Poetry Daily, Verse Daily, Fungi Magazine and Mothering Magazine. He lives in Trout Lake, Colorado.

www.ingramcontent.com/pod-product-compliance
Lightning Source LLC
Chambersburg PA
CBHW032236080426
42735CB00008B/874